THE GRATITUDE JOURNAL

A 21-DAY CHALLENGE TO MORE GRATITUDE, DEEPER RELATIONSHIPS, AND GREATER JOY

Shelley Hitz

Printed in the United States of America
ISBN: 978-1-946118-08-0

Edited by Shannon Janeczek: www.publishsavvy.com

CONTENTS

THE GRATITUDE JOURNAL

Welcome to this 21-day journey toward more gratitude, deeper relationships, and more joy. I am so excited you have decided to join us in taking this gratitude challenge.

Gratitude is powerful and has the potential to transform your life. It has changed mine!

As you go through this 21-day challenge, I encourage you to keep a journal. You can write directly in this book or you can start a journal online, in a notebook, or use our printable gratitude journal that accompanies this book.

Go and download the printable journal we have designed as a companion to this book for FREE here: http://shelleyhitz.com/freegratitudejournal

I encourage you to commit the next 21 days to this challenge. Each day you will read an entry in this book, write in your gratitude journal, and send a thank you card to someone in your life. If you miss a day, don't give up. Start where you left off and continue the challenge.

Thank you for joining me on this journey. I truly do appreciate you!

DAY #1

THANKFULNESS. GRATITUDE. CONTENTMENT.

These are words that are familiar to us, especially those of us that call ourselves followers of Jesus.

And yet, how often do we get stuck in the opposite?

Self-Pity. Complaining. Discontentment.

I have to admit that I've been there lately. I've been through so many changes recently and some people might think that I have it made. Others might think I'm crazy. But, I don't think many realize how difficult it has been for me.

The Changes in My Life Over the Last Year

I resigned my job as a Physical Therapist last July to minister and work full-time with my husband CJ.

This is a dream we have been working towards ever since we came back from serving as short-term missionaries in Belize. When we returned, we had thousands of dollars of debt, which (in my thinking), forced me back to my job as a physical therapist. Although the job was rewarding and paid well, it was not what we felt God called us to in this season of our lives. After ministering together and working together for two years in Belize, we sensed that was what we were to continue to do.

However, it was seven years later that we were finally able to pay off all our consumer debt. Being debt-free (except for our mortgage) allowed me to resign my job as a physical therapist and embark once again into ministering and working full-time together. What a great feeling it was to pay off our debt!

And yet the transition has been harder for me than I anticipated.

I had become dependent on the regular paychecks and benefits that came with my job. And I realized that I received some of my self-worth from my job title. People instantly respected me as a physical therapist, whereas I get very different reactions when I tell someone I am an "author and speaker." It's almost as if people want to ask, "Oh really? What is your REAL job?"

God is teaching me to gain my worth from who I am in HIM, not what I do. But it's been a hard transition. We also went from living in a 1300 square-foot home to a 125 square-foot RV, to living in my mom's spare bedroom, then finally settling in Colorado Springs.

What a ride!

I wouldn't go back and do anything different, as God has used these months of transition in our lives to help us grow. But, after months of living out of bags and moving from place to place, I am ready to "nest" again and be settled in ONE place.

When we moved out of our house into our RV, we had to get rid of a lot of stuff. If I would have known that just a few months later we would be moving into a condo in Colorado Springs, I probably would have kept some of the things I gave away. But the experience taught me a lot about living simply. I realized that I truly didn't need all that material stuff. When it really came down to it, I truly only needed a very small amount of material possessions and was able to live without much.

Findlay, Ohio, was a place I called home for over 20 years. We moved there when I was a junior in high school in 1991, and except for college and our time in Belize, Findlay, has been home. All my family lives in Ohio, and so to move over 1200 miles away was both exciting and sad.

A Season of New Things in My Life, But Also a Season of Grieving

And here I sit. Although there have been a lot of exciting changes in my life, it's also been a season of grieving.

- Grieving the loss of my job, career, and what I thought I would be doing for the rest of my life.
- Grieving the loss of our first house and a lot of the material stuff that filled it.
- Grieving the loss of my home of 20 years and living close to my family.

Sometimes we can get stuck in the grief. God has felt distant to me throughout these changes, so sometimes I feel alone and stuck in self-pity. Poor me. Why can't I live a normal life like most people?

It is Important to Grieve

I was reminded that it is important to grieve, even the little things that don't seem important at the time. My mom always says, it is important to feel your feelings and then let them pass, surrendering them into the hands of Jesus so that they don't get stuck or bottled up within us.

And so I have allowed myself to grieve. Even as I've written this book, I've cried a few tears. For me, tears can be healing.

I Felt Stuck

Yet, as I began to process some of my emotions, I felt stuck. I had given into the habit of working long hours on both ministry and business projects. I believe workaholism is one of my last addictions from which Christ is now working to set me free.

It is an acceptable addiction in the church and in our culture. It is even often praised.

- Great job, Shelley.
- Wow, you're a real workhorse.
- Look at all you've accomplished.

You get the picture.

It was also my way of trying, in self-sufficiency, to provide financially for our needs. I felt the burden of providing in this way after I quit my physical therapy job. I felt the need to replace the income I was giving up when I resigned my job, but I also wanted to do whatever I needed to ensure I wouldn't need to work a 9-to-5 job again. I wanted to have the freedom to continue to minister with CJ as God opens the doors, as well as work from home when, in God's timing, we start a family. We are praying that this happens sooner rather than later, but again, we're trusting God's timing.

Self-sufficiency and workaholism run rampant in our culture. It's so easy to get caught up in the rat race. We keep ourselves so busy. Even after resigning my job, there were often many times I would work 12-hour days. I am very driven and joked with my jusband CJ that I was working harder than I ever did in my physical therapy job.

Praying for Freedom and Contentment

So here I am. Praying for freedom from the unbalanced life I created. Praying for freedom from the self-sufficiency and workaholism deeply rooted in my life. Praying for contentment in my circumstances.

Then I had a friend email me and say she was praying for accountability in a certain area, and the only person that came to her mind was me. I agreed to do this for her, and asked if she would also help keep me accountable in my workaholism and my attempt at living a more balanced life. She agreed, and I believe God is providing for both of us in this way. Even though we are thousands of miles apart, we are keeping each other accountable via email on a daily basis and praying for each other. God has provided accountability for me in other areas of my life just when I needed it, and I believe He is providing it for me again.

One of Our Greatest Weapons as Christians is a Spirit of Thankfulness and Gratitude

Another thing God keeps bringing to my mind is the topics of thankfulness and gratitude. I am reminded that thankfulness and gratitude are the opposite of self-pity and a complaining spirit.

I know, I know. It seems like a pat answer: "Just be thankful for what you have," or, "Give thanks in all things." But, there is POWER in being thankful, even when you don't FEEL like being thankful.

I remembered a book I started to read in a Barnes and Noble bookstore one day about a man who wrote thank you notes every day for one year. It wasn't a Christian book, but it demonstrated the power of being intentionally thankful. I believe it is a Biblical concept that can be experienced by anyone who practices it.

And then I remembered people who I've seen post on Facebook or their blogs something they are thankful for every day for a series of days. I felt led to do something similar and remembered that…

It Takes 21 Days to Start a New Habit

Many people say it takes 21 days to start a new habit or break an old one. Whether it is getting in the habit of exercising, eating right or developing a spirit of thankfulness.

And so I decided to take a 21-Day Gratitude Challenge.

21 Days of Gratitude

What does this mean? It can mean different things for different people. But, for me, I sense that I need to take the initiative to write down the things and people in my life that I am grateful for in my journal for the next 21 days. At the same time, I will choose one person each day to write a handwritten thank you note. In the note, I will share why I am thankful for them and send it via postal mail.

I found 21 thank-you notes and cards in my closet, got them out and wrote my first thank-you note today. Then, I got out my journal that has been somewhat neglected over the past few months and wrote out three specific things that I am thankful for in my life in these three categories: spiritual, physical and relational. I wrote several sentences of what I am thankful for and why in each category.

Already I can feel the direction of my heart changing. Imagine what will happen after 21 days of being intentionally thankful for all I've been given.

Because I've been given a lot, more than I deserve.

And it's time to not allow satan to keep me in the grips of self-pity, a complaining attitude, and discontentment. I am asking God to bring breakthrough in my heart through the power of His Holy Spirit as I take these intentional steps toward gratitude.

Will You Join Me?

What about you? Will you consider joining me in these 21 days of gratitude? It may look different for you and that's okay. Simply ask God what He wants you to do and then do it. It may be as simple as saying out loud one thing you are thankful for each day. Or like me, you may decide to write physical thank-you notes and send them in the mail each day.

If you feel stuck in self-pity or discontentment, I challenge you to join me. Ask the Holy Spirit to change you as you take simple steps of intentional gratitude in your life. Watch and see what God does.

"Appreciation is the highest form of prayer, for it acknowledges the presence of good wherever you shine the light of your thankful thoughts." ~ Alan Cohen

"Enter into His gates with thanksgiving, And into His courts with praise. Be thankful to Him, and bless His name." ~ Psalm 100:4 (NKJV)

Application: If you are ready to take this challenge with me and want to share the journey with others, join our private Facebook group here: www.bodyandsoulpublishing.com/gratitudegroup

Once you are there, I encourage you to post something you are grateful for each day for 21 days. You can also post stories of how God is working in your life through the gratitude challenge.

Download our free printable gratitude journal or you can write directly in this book. Personally, I chose three categories to write something I'm thankful for each day: spiritual, physical and relational. I also wrote a handwritten thank-you card to someone different each day of my 21 days of gratitude challenge.

Whatever, you do, I encourage you to spend time focusing on all that God has given you.

TODAY I AM GRATEFUL FOR:

1. _____

2. _____

3. _____

DAY #2

As part of the challenge, I've decided to write a handwritten thank-you note each day to someone in my life that I appreciate. Not an email, text or Facebook message but an actual card that I send in the mail. There is something special that happens when you write out your thoughts with pen and paper. Plus, it's more meaningful to the receiver, because how often do you receive a card in the mail anymore?

"Nothing is more honorable than a grateful heart."
~ Shakespeare

"I thank my God upon every remembrance of you."
~ Philippians 1:3 (KJV)

Application: I encourage you to send someone you appreciate in your life a handwritten thank-you note today. Even if you don't have cards to write on, use the paper you have and send a thoughtful note to brighten someone's day!

TODAY I AM GRATEFUL FOR:

1. _____

2. _____

3._____

DAY #3

I've started using an outline in my journal as I write out the things I'm thankful for each day in the three categories I've chosen: spiritual, physical and relational. I also make a note of who I wrote a thank-you card to that day and why. You can see the outline in the picture above.

As I wrote my thank-you note today, I had tears in my eyes. Not tears of sadness, but tears of joy and gratitude for all this person has done for me. It was a special moment remembering the many things I have to be thankful for today. I would not have experienced this if I had not been purposefully writing out thank-you notes to people I appreciate in my life.

"You say, 'If I had a little more, I should be satisfied.' You made a mistake. If you are not content with what you have, you would not be satisfied if it were doubled." ~ Charles Haddon Spurgeon

"I know what it is to be in need, and I know what it is to have plenty. I have learned the secret of being content in any and every situation, whether well fed or hungry, whether living in plenty or in want. I can do all this through him who gives me strength."
~ Philippians 4:12-13 (NIV)

Application: Decide on an outline you want to use and start writing what you are thankful for each day in this book.

TODAY I AM GRATEFUL FOR:

1. _____

2. _____

3._____

DAY #4

There are some days that are more difficult to find something to be thankful for in our lives. However, the more we foster an attitude of gratitude, the more it gets our focus off of the negativity around us. As my parents used to always say, "Your glass is either half full or half empty, it just depends on how you see your life."

I'm choosing to see my glass full right now and it is changing me.

"We ought to give thanks for all the fortune: if it is 'good,' be-cause it is good, if 'bad' because it works in us patience, humili-ty, and the contempt of this world and the hope of our eternal country." ~ C.S. Lewis

"Be thankful in all circumstances, for this is God's will for you who belong to Christ Jesus."
~ 1 Thessalonians 5:18 (NLT)

Application: Ask God to help you see the times in your day when you are looking at your life as half-empty and complaining about the circumstances around you. When you realize this, ask God to help you give that concern to Him in prayer and instead find something to be thankful for at that time.

Even if it is something we normally take for granted, like our eyesight, or ability to taste food, there is always something to be thankful for in all circumstances.

TODAY I AM GRATEFUL FOR:

1. _____

2. _____

3._____

DAY #5

To be honest, today was hard for me to complete. I got busy with the day and tasks on hand that I didn't finish my journal entry until the end of the day. For me, it's not about being legalistic about what I do in this challenge (write a thank-you note each day, and write in my journal three things I'm thankful for), but about putting Christ first in my life and in my thoughts. Unfortunately, I don't feel like I put Him first today and I could feel the internal struggle all day long.

What God has taught me over and over again is that when I put Him first, everything else will fall into place. Matthew 6:33 says it so perfectly, "But seek first his kingdom and his righteousness, and all these things will be given to you as well." (NIV)

And so, today as I asked God for forgiveness for putting other things ahead of Him. I'm thankful for His forgiveness that washes me white as snow whenever I confess my sins to Him.

"Come now, let us settle the matter," says the Lord. "Though your sins are like scarlet, they shall be as white as snow; though they are red as crimson, they shall be like wool."~ Isaiah 1:8 (NIV)

Application: Ask God if there is anything in your heart that is keeping you from an attitude of gratitude. Confess your sin to him and thank him for cleansing you white as snow.

TODAY I AM GRATEFUL FOR:

1. _____

2. _____

3._____

DAY #6

As I was writing a thank-you card today, I was thinking about some good reasons to send a thank-you card. There are many reasons, but here are just a few:

1. Thank someone for a gift they gave you (Christmas, birthday).
2. Thank someone for something they did for you (watched your kids while you were at a meeting, mowed your lawn, brought you food).
3. Thank someone for hosting you at their home (for dinner, overnight).
4. Thank someone for brightening your day (a salesperson who was exceptionally helpful, a co-worker that encouraged you).
5. Thank someone for being in your life. This is a great opportunity to thank those we take most for granted (husband/wife, mother/father, siblings, children).

Those are just a few ideas to get you started. I'm sure you can think of many more!

"If we pause to think, we'll have cause to thank."
~ Unknown

"We give thanks to the God and Father of our Lord Jesus Christ, praying always for you, since we heard of your faith in Christ Jesus and of your love for all the saints." ~ Colossians 1:3-4 (NKJV)

Application: What are some other reasons you can think of for sending thank-you cards? Write out at least two more reasons of your own and then send a thank-you card to someone in your life.

TODAY I AM GRATEFUL FOR:

1. _____

2. _____

3._____

DAY #7

It's hard to believe it's been a week since I first started this challenge. One week down, two to go. I'm realizing more than ever that what Henri Nouwen says in the quote below is so true:

"Gratitude...goes beyond the 'mine' and 'thine' and claims the truth that all of life is a pure gift. In the past I always thought of gratitude as a spontaneous response to the awareness of gifts received, but now I realize that gratitude can also be lived as a discipline. The discipline of gratitude is the explicit effort to acknowledge that all I am and have is given to me as a gift of love, a gift to be celebrated with joy." ~ Henri J.M. Nouwen

"And we also thank God continually because, when you received the word of God, which you heard from us, you accepted it not as a human word, but as it actually is, the word of God, which is indeed at work in you who believe." ~ I Thessalonians 2:13 (NIV)

Application: Look up the word thanks and thanksgiving in the Bible using a concordance or www.biblegateway.com. Then, choose one verse to memorize.

TODAY I AM GRATEFUL FOR:

1. _____

2. _____

3._____

DAY #8

Yesterday was hard and I felt myself sinking into self-pity again. All my efforts to try to find something to be thankful for fell short, because I was trying to fight a spiritual battle in my own strength. It wasn't until we attended a church service last night that I began to feel a breakthrough. I cried almost the entire worship service as the Holy Spirit ministered to me.

I still have to fight the battle each day, but God reminded me that He has given us the victory over any darkness that threatens to overtake us through Jesus Christ.

"But thanks be to God, who gives us the victory through our Lord Jesus Christ." ~ 1 Corinthians 15:57 (NKJV)

"Gratitude is the least of the virtues, but ingratitude is the worst of vices." ~ Thomas Fuller

Application: Thank Jesus today for the victory he has given you over self-pity and an ungrateful, complaining spirit.

Ask for the empowerment of His Spirit to help you overcome any darkness that threatens you today.

TODAY I AM GRATEFUL FOR:

1. _____

2. _____

3. _____

DAY #9

Today I wrote a thank-you note to my Grandpa ("PawPaw"), who is now 96 and served in the Army in World War II. I'm so thankful that God preserved his life, as I would not be here otherwise.

"Thanksgiving is recognition of a debt that cannot be paid. We express thanks, whether or not we are able otherwise to reimburse the giver. When thanksgiving is filled with true meaning and is not just the formality of a polite 'thank you,' it is the recognition of dependence." ~ Billy Graham

"So we, Your people and sheep of Your pasture, will give You thanks forever; We will show forth Your praise to all generations." ~ Psalm 79:13 (NKJV)

Application: Send a thank-you note to someone you know that has served or is serving in the military.

TODAY I AM GRATEFUL FOR:

1. _____

2. _____

3. _____

DAY #10

So many times the things we complain about are things that God has already given us. We just need to come to him and 'cash the check' He has already given us.

Corrie ten Boom is one of my heroes and role models in this life. She was a Nazi concentration camp survivor that God used in amazing ways through her writing and speaking as she traveled around the world.

As I was reading in her book, "Amazing Love" this morning, this quote impacted me, "The Bible is a checkbook. When you said yes to Jesus Christ, many promises were deposited to your credit at that very moment, and they were signed by the Lord Jesus Himself. But now you have to cash your checks in order to profit by them. When you come upon such a promise and say, 'Thank you, Lord, I accept this,' then you have cashed a check, and that very day you'll be richer than you were the day before."

I encourage you to read Corrie's analogy, then ask God how He wants you to apply it to your life today.

"Blessed be the God and Father of our Lord Jesus Christ, who has blessed us with every spiritual blessing in the heavenly places in Christ." ~ Ephesians 1:3 (NKJV)

Application: Write out at least five spiritual blessings you have been given through Christ. Thank Him for those blessings today by saying, "Thank you Lord, I accept this blessing."

TODAY I AM GRATEFUL FOR:

1. _____

2. _____

3. _____

DAY #11

"Feeling gratitude and not expressing it is like wrapping a present and not giving it."
~ William Arthur Ward

"Make a joyful shout to the Lord, all you lands!
Serve the Lord with gladness;
Come before His presence with singing.
Know that the Lord, He is God;
It is He who has made us, and not we ourselves;
We are His people and the sheep of His pasture.
Enter into His gates with thanksgiving,
And into His courts with praise.
Be thankful to Him, and bless His name.
For the Lord is good;
His mercy is everlasting,
And His truth endures to all generations."
~ Psalm 100 (NKJV)

Application: One way to express our gratitude to God is through worship music. Play a worship song and sing along or sing a song to the Lord to express your thanks to Him today.

TODAY I AM GRATEFUL FOR:

1. _____

2. _____

3._____

DAY #12

"Today, when stress mounts, I pray to dismount it with gratitude. I can only feel one feeling at a time, and I choose to give thanks at all times. Fight feeling with feeling!" ~ Ann Voskamp

"Be anxious for nothing, but in everything by prayer and supplication, with thanksgiving, let your requests be made known to God; and the peace of God, which surpasses all understanding, will guard your hearts and minds through Christ Jesus."~ Philippians 4:6-7 (NKJV)

Application: What are you anxious about today? Choose to pray about the situation instead of worry and complain.

Find one thing that you can be thankful for about the situation and pray a prayer of thanksgiving as well. Even if your heart isn't in it at first, take the step of faith and see what God does.

TODAY I AM GRATEFUL FOR:

1. _____

2. _____

3._____

DAY #13

I'm only on day 13 and yet I'm finding it harder and harder to think of someone new to send a handwritten thank-you card to each day. However, as I took some time to reflect on all I've been given today, I was able to think of another person that blessed us, and so another card was written, addressed, stamped and sent out in the mail.

I have heard that writing something out in a journal (or writing cards like I am each day) does something deeper within us than just saying the words or typing them out. I don't know the exact reason, but I do know that you involve more senses as you write: your senses of touch and sight. And I do think there is value in writing things out.

For example, as I write out three things I'm thankful for each day in my journal and a handwritten thank-you card, it deepens my focus on the things I am thankful for today. It also leaves a record that I can look back upon when I need the encouragement.

"Hear, O Israel: The Lord our God, the Lord is one! You shall love the Lord your God with all your heart, with all your soul, and with all your strength. And these words which I command you today shall be in your heart. You shall teach them diligently to your children, and shall talk of them when you sit in your house, when you walk by the way, when you lie down, and when you rise up. You shall bind them as a sign on your hand, and they shall be as frontlets between your eyes. You shall write them on the doorposts of your house and on your gates." ~ Deuteronomy 6: 4-9 (NKJV)

"Gratitude to God makes even a temporal blessing a taste of heaven." ~ Wm. Romaine

Application: Write out what you are thankful for today below. I encourage you to write it out as a prayer to God,: "Thank you Lord for _____ today because _____."

TODAY I AM GRATEFUL FOR:

1. _____

2. _____

3._____

DAY #14

"A thankful heart enjoys blessings twice – when they're received, and when they're remembered."
~ Unknown

"And give thanks for everything to God the Father in the name of our Lord Jesus Christ." ~ Ephesians 5:20 (NLT)

Application: Learn to enjoy your blessings twice.

TODAY I AM GRATEFUL FOR:

1. _____

2. _____

3. _____

DAY #15

"Ingratitude is always a form of weakness. I have never known a man of real ability to be ungrateful." ~ Goethe

Even Jesus displayed a spiritual of gratefulness to His Father.

"So they rolled the stone aside. Then Jesus looked up to heaven and said, 'Father, thank you for hearing me. You always hear me, but I said it out loud for the sake of all these people standing here, so that they will believe you sent me.'" ~ John 11:41-42 (NLT)

<u>Application:</u> Think of the people of real ability in your life. Do they display an attitude of gratefulness or a complaining spirit? Which do you want to be known for in your life? Let's follow the example of Jesus and display thankfulness in our lives.

TODAY I AM GRATEFUL FOR:

1. _____

2. _____

3._____

DAY #16

I had tears in my eyes after watching this video, "The Amazing Story of Ian and Larissa," that my friend, Renee, recommended to me: http://www.godtube.com/watch/?v=WLDGDGNX.. In the video, they show how they created a gratitude board to remind them of what they are thankful for each day. I then decided to follow their example and create a gratitude board in our house. Thankfully, my husband agreed.

"Cultivate a thankful spirit! It will be to thee a perpetual feast. There is, or ought to be, with us no such thing as small mercies; all are great, because the least are undeserved. Indeed, a really thankful heart will extract motive for gratitude from every-thing, making the most even of scanty blessings." ~ J.R. MacDuff

"Therefore I exhort first of all that supplications, prayers, intercessions, and giving of thanks be made for all men." ~ I Timothy 2:1 (NKJV)

<u>Application:</u> Consider starting a gratitude board of your own. It could be simple; anything you want it to be. For example, you can write something that you are thankful for that day on your mirror with a dry erase marker. Here are a few other examples of what you can use to create your gratitude board:

- Mirror
- Chalkboard
- Dry erase board
- Poster board
- Corkboard
- Or use sticky notes

It is a tangible way to keep your focus on all that you have to be grateful for each day. If you want to use the heading and quotes I used on our board, you can download them and print them off here: http://gratitude.s3.amazonaws.com/gratitude-board.pdf

TODAY I AM GRATEFUL FOR:

1. _____

2. _____

3. _____

DAY #17

Wow, it is hard to believe that today is already day 17 in the gratitude challenge. Only 4 more days left, but already God has blessed me through taking the time to focus on Him and all that He has given me.

Instead of being down and indulging in self-pity about being in a new place without a church home or friends, I have been focused on all that He has given me. In the process, I am watching as He is providing relationships for me, as well as community with other believers. How amazing is that? Thank you, Lord, for providing what I need, as I trust you and keep my focus on all that You've given me.

"If you have a special need today, focus your full attention on the goodness and greatness of your Father rather than on the size of your need. Your need is tiny compared to His ability to meet it." ~ Bill Patterson

"If you, then, though you are evil, know how to give good gifts to your children, how much more will your

Father in heaven give good gifts to those who ask him!" ~ Matthew 7:11 (NIV)

"And my God will meet all your needs according to his glorious riches in Christ Jesus." ~ Philippians 4:19 (NIV)

Application: Instead of focusing on the biggest need in your life today, focus on Christ and what He has given you. Every time that big need comes to mind and threatens to take over, surrender it again to Jesus, thanking Him for providing the answer even before you can see your prayer answered. Trust that He will provide everything you need.

TODAY I AM GRATEFUL FOR:

1. _____

2. _____

3._____

DAY #18

I have a friend, Katie Marie Rowden, who says one way God romances her is to show her hearts everywhere: heart-shaped rocks, heart-shaped dirt clots, etc. She has a Facebook group for women where she and others post ways God romances them each day.

I have been walking and jogging along the same path for the last six weeks and until two days ago, I didn't notice ANY hearts. Then, all of a sudden I started to see hearts everywhere. Yesterday I decided to take some pictures. There were so many more that I didn't stop to capture.

Originally, I had felt like looking for hearts was Katie's thing, but yesterday I sensed God saying it was also His way of showing me today how much He loves me and is providing for me, which He is! So, as I was walking along seeing rocks that resembled hearts and feeling loved by my Savior, I prayed and asked God if He would show me a rock that was almost perfectly shaped as a heart, and He did!! I'm feeling very loved today.

As I'm in the middle of this 21-day gratitude challenge, God reminded me yesterday that you find what you look for in life. When we were looking at purchasing a Toyota RV, I suddenly saw them everywhere. After we bought our car, I saw the same make and model everywhere.

Just like seeing these hearts today along my running path that have been there all along, when we look for something to be thankful for in our life, we'll find it. However, when we look for the negative in our lives, we'll find it as well. It's all a matter of what you are looking for.

Application: Is your focus currently on your problems or on Jesus and all that He has given you today? I encourage you to look for something to be thankful for today!

"The longer I live, the more I realize the impact of attitude on life. Attitude, to me, is more important than facts. It is more important than the past, the education, the money, than circumstances, than failure, than successes, than what other people think or say or do. It is more important than appearance, giftedness or skill. It will make or break a company... a church...a home.

The remarkable thing is we have a choice everyday regarding the attitude we will embrace for that day. We cannot change our past...we cannot change the fact that people will act in a certain way. We cannot change the inevitable. The only thing we can do is play on the one string we have, and that is our attitude.

I am convinced that life is 10% what happens to me and 90% of how I react to it. And so it is with you... we are in charge of our attitudes." ~ Charles R. Swindoll

"Therefore we also, since we are surrounded by so great a cloud of witnesses, let us lay aside every weight, and the sin which so easily ensnares us, and let us run with endurance the race that is set before us, looking unto Jesus, the author and finisher of our faith, who for the joy that was set before Him endured the cross, despising the shame, and has sat down at the right hand of the throne of God." ~ Hebrews 12:1-2 (NKJV)

TODAY I AM GRATEFUL FOR:

1. _____

2. _____

3._____

DAY #19

At the same time that I'm taking this gratitude challenge, I'm also working on having better balance in my life and not allowing workaholism or negative emotions to dominate.

I have had better balance and am so thankful for that breakthrough. However, yesterday I was thinking about some upcoming project deadlines that I have and began to freak out, wondering how I was going to get it all done.

I was on a day trip with my husband when this tsunami of negative emotions threatened to ruin my day. Even in the midst of beautiful scenery on an amazing hike (see the picture on the next page), emotions like worry, anxiety, fear, or a complaining spirit started to descend upon me.

Then, I began to sense God asking me to change my focus. Instead of complaining about all that I have to do, I started thanking God for the opportunities He has given me. It wasn't an instant change, but it did help, and gradually my focus re-turned again to God

and not my deadlines. I then began to pray and ask God for wisdom on how to accomplish all that is on my plate. Throughout the day, I realized that two of my projects had self-imposed deadlines that I could delay if needed. Then I didn't feel so overwhelmed anymore.

I remember a friend of mine saying that she struggled with picking up her husband's dirty socks on their bedroom floor and doing laundry for her family. She found herself grumbling and complaining about it on almost a daily basis. And yet, she sensed God asking her to change her perspective.

Instead of complaining about picking up dirty socks, she started thanking God that she has a husband to pick up socks for, a husband that provides for her and loves her. And instead of complaining about doing her children's laundry, she would thank God that she has children to wash clothes for, children that are healthy and that add so much to her life.

It sounds easy, right?

But, when our emotions start to take over, it no longer feels so easy to be thankful. However, what I found out yesterday is that if you take the step of faith and start thanking God in your situation, even when you don't yet feel thankful, it can change you and your entire day!

Application: Don't give into the negative emotions that want to take you under today. I encourage you to identify one thing that you often find yourself complaining about in your life. Then, ask God for at least one thing you can be thankful for in that situation, and when tempted to complain, allow gratitude to be on your lips instead.

"It is impossible to feel grateful and depressed in the same moment." ~ Naomi Williams

"Since we are receiving a Kingdom that is unshakable, let us be thankful and please God by worshiping him with holy fear and awe." ~ Hebrews 12:28 (NLT)

TODAY I AM GRATEFUL FOR:

1. _____

2. _____

3._____

DAY #20

I thought that today as my 21-day gratitude challenge winds down, I would share several quotes that relate to being thankful and living a life filled with gratitude.

<u>Application:</u> Choose one of the quotes below that impacts you the most and write it out on a note card or sticky note. Put the quote somewhere where you will see it every day.

"The unthankful heart discovers no mercies; but the thankful heart will find, in every hour, some heavenly blessings." ~ Henry Ward Beecher

"Gratitude shouldn't be an occasional incident but a continuous attitude." ~ Anthony Nyuiemedy-Adiase

"The hardest arithmetic to master is that which enables us to count our blessings." ~ Eric Hoffer

"Pride slays thanksgiving, but a humble mind is the soil out of which thanks naturally grows. A proud man is seldom a grateful man, for he never thinks he gets as much as he deserves." ~ Henry Ward Beecher

"We prevent God from giving us the great spiritual gifts He has in store for us, because we do not give thanks for daily gifts. We think we dare not be satisfied with the small measure of spiritual knowledge, experience, and love that has been given to us...We pray for the big things and forget to give thanks for the ordinary, small (and yet really not small) gifts. How can God entrust great things to one who will not thankfully receive from Him the little things?"
~ Dietrich Bonhoeffer

"If you can't be content with what you have received, be thankful for what you have escaped." ~ Author unknown

"God gave you a gift of 86,400 seconds today. Have you used one to say 'thank you'?" ~ William A. Ward

"I thank God for my handicaps, for, through them, I have found myself, my work and my God." ~ Helen Keller

TODAY I AM GRATEFUL FOR:

1. _____

2. _____

3. _____

DAY #21

Wow, it's hard to believe it is day 21 already. Three weeks. It went by so fast and yet God has done a lot of work in my heart over these last 21 days. I know it is just the beginning as a life of gratitude is like a garden. It takes an intentional effort to cultivate. Just like a garden, when we begin to neglect our relationship with Jesus and allow negativity to creep in, it is like weeds growing and choking out the life-giving plants. The "weeds" that can grow in our garden of gratitude are self-pity, a complaining spirit, and a negative attitude. And if we aren't careful, these weeds can soon take over our entire garden.

However, I have seen God begin to uproot some of these weeds in my heart over the last 21 days, and water the life-giving plants in my heart. He has done the work in my heart; it was nothing that I could do on my own through self-help or self-effort.

And as I've surrendered myself to God, confessed my sin of a negative attitude and taken intentional steps of gratitude, some amazing things have happened. We have started to make friends and find community among other believers in a church in our new location. However, life is not perfect and I still have struggles from day to day. And yet God is helping me to see things from a different perspective.

Seeing From a Different Perspective

As I was thinking about this yesterday, God immediately brought an illustration to my mind. Have you ever seen optical illusions that look like one thing, but really are another?

I found a couple to share with you. The first is an illusion created by Edward H. Adelson, Professor of Vision Science at MIT. Believe it or not, Box A and Box B are the exact same color in the picture below. Hard to believe, right? But, it's true! I even checked it with my graphics program, Adobe Photoshop, and

Edward H. Adelson

sure enough each box comes up as the EXACT same color, #787878.

And it reminded me that often times, as followers of Jesus, we look at our circumstances and see our life differently than what is really true. Our enemy, satan, is the father of all lies, and many times presents a situation to us that, like the picture above, looks different than it really is. And instead of seeing the truth of how blessed we are or all the spiritual blessings God showers upon us each day, we see only the negative and how we wish things could be different. Another example is in the picture below. What word do you see?

Did you see good or evil? The word good is written in black, whereas the word evil is written inside the letters in white.

It's all a matter of perspective of what we choose to focus on, right? And the same is true in our lives. If we are looking for it, we can always see the evil in our lives and the negative. However, when looking at the same circumstances we can also see the good in our lives and all that God has given us.

As our 21-day gratitude challenge comes to an end, I pray that God empowers us through His Holy Spirit to continue to see the good in our lives and circumstances. And that we continue to cultivate our garden of gratitude each day and not let the weeds overtake it ever again.

Application: What are you focusing on today in your life? The good or the evil? I encourage you to focus on all that God has given you today. It's all a matter of perspective.

"The optimist says, the cup is half full. The pessimist says, the cup is half empty. The child of God says; My cup runneth over." ~ Anonymous

"My [brimming] cup runs over." ~ Psalm 23:5 (AMPC)

"The Lord is my shepherd; I shall not want. He makes me to lie down in green pastures; He leads me beside the still waters. He restores my soul; He leads me in the paths of righteousness For His name's sake. Yea, though I walk through the valley of the shadow of death, I will fear no evil; For You are with me;

Your rod and Your staff, they comfort me. You prepare a table be-fore me in the presence of my enemies; You anoint my head with oil; My cup runs over. Surely goodness and mercy shall follow me All the days of my life; And I will dwell in the house of the Lord Forever." ~ Psalm 23 (NKJV)

TODAY I AM GRATEFUL FOR:

1. _____

2. _____

3. _____

OTHERS' STORIES

I wanted to share some stories from those who joined our Facebook group and decided to take the 21 Days of Gratitude Challenge.

Rob Stephens: I praise God for giving me this opportunity to share, to see others share, to unite with other God-fearing people, and most of all to develop a closer relationship with an awesome God! This has made me think of Him more, what He does for me and what He does for others. All of this states the fact that He loves us and all He wants us to do is love Him back!

I haven't been to church or even had a Bible for over three years, and this challenge has brought me back to Him in such a way I cannot explain with words! 21days, it would be a pleasure to do this challenge for 21 years! Thank you, Lord, for giving us this way to bring us closer to You! What an awesome God we serve! AMEN!

Laurie MacPherson: This gratitude challenge is spreading! Right now my mom and I are talking about gratitude and faith, something she really needs right now. We recently lost my Dad, and it has been hard for us, especially my mama. Now we're having an excellent conversation. This challenge has been quite an inspiration. Keep up the great work. It's contagious! Wow!

David Rickey: I want to share what this Gratitude Challenge has done for me since I have started. I am on day 13 and I can honestly say this has made me think about every single way I go about life. It has brought to my attention on how much I complain about the tiniest of things when I have such a blessed and fulfilled life. It has also taught me that I have so many things to be thankful for. It has helped me find happiness in life I haven't had in a while.

I think everyone should do this challenge if they haven't yet. You will be blessed.

Another thing this challenge has done is to bring me closer with the big guy upstairs, my true father, my Jesus, my provider, my everything. I feel like since I have started this God and I have started to kindle an intimate relationship with each other that I have never experienced before; it's something that no human or woman can ever give me on this earth, and it is something that will never be taken from me. All I want to do is draw closer to you, God. That is my only desire, since I have started this. Bless you everybody and I hope you get as much out of this as I did.

Renee Snyder: The gratitude challenge has been life-changing for me. I usually post in the early part of the day. That helps me to get my mind and heart focused on good things to start the day off well! It has also helped me to identify what I need to talk with the Lord about when I recognize negative thoughts and attitudes I am having. Doing this daily has drawn me clos-er to the Lord because I am communicating with him more about real heart and thought issues in real time. In other words, I'm not just overlooking what is going on inside of me and letting my feelings about circumstances rule the day. I was able to realize that my thoughts hold the reins to my feelings. What I think, and what I feel as a result, affects my behavior. Now I recognize that I can lead my feelings by choosing my thoughts! I was putting the cart (my feelings) before the horse (my thinking) before. I think that's what negativity is. Our feelings ruling our thoughts.

Also, being mindful to be grateful has helped me to hear his voice better. It's like my radio tuner finally found the station. That surprised me a lot. I didn't realize that my bad attitudes had clogged my hearing so much. The other day, I allowed negativity to rule the day and it was so much more obvious that I had lost my peace. This made it easier to change my mind about the way I was dealing with things, ask for the Lord's help, and get back on course.

I intend to make this a lifestyle, because through experiencing the changes in my life, I understand why the word of God tells us "For the rest, brethren, whatever is true, whatever is worthy of reverence and is honorable and seemly, whatever is just, whatever is pure, whatever is lovely and lovable, whatever is kind and winsome and gracious, if there is any virtue and ex-cellence, if there is anything worthy of praise, think on and weigh and take account of these things [fix your minds on them]." ~ Philippians 4:8 (AMPC)

Philippians 4:4-9 is the passage that really locks in the whole idea of gratitude for me.

I am so thankful that the Lord prompted Shelley to share this challenge with all of us! Above all, I praise Jesus for his grace in providing us all a way to be mindful of the thoughts and attitudes of our hearts, and to experience the difference that gratitude makes in our lives! Gratitude opens the door to God's grace, joy, and peace!

Antonia Faisant: I really appreciated the Gratitude Challenge because not only was it confirmation concerning what the Lord has been speaking to me about, but it also solidified my need for it. I really enjoyed sharing, but also loved being encouraged by others and the things they were thankful for each day. I really enjoyed the scripture verses and the application. I think my absolute favorite thing was the gratitude board. This is something that I would like to do as well, because then it becomes a lifelong discipline.

This challenge has really changed my focus from the negative things in life and to focus on the good. I believe a thankful heart is a happy heart. Proverbs 17:22 says, "A cheerful heart is good medicine, but a crushed spirit dries up the bones." (NIV)

Join us here:
www.bodyandsoulpublishing.com/gratitudegroup

21 PRAYERS OF GRATITTUDE

Prayer changes things. It changes me. When I pray consistently to God, something changes within me. However, sometimes it is easy to get caught up in the busyness of life and not take the time to pray.

We do not have to pray in a certain way for God to hear us. We can simply lift up the prayer of our hearts to Him as if we are talking with a friend. However, in this book, I have taken key truths from scripture and reworded them into prayers of gratitude. Combining prayer with God's Word is powerful.

I have experienced this in my own life and now want to share it with you.

They say it takes 21 days to form a new habit. And so I have shared 21 prayers of gratitude with you to help you form a habit of prayer in your life. I pray that these prayers help you to overcome negativity through applying the power of prayer and God's Word to your life. I also pray that when you finish this book, your prayers will continue on your own. I encourage you to dig into God's Word and come up with your own prayers.

If you are struggling in a certain area, I recommend using a concordance or an online tool like BibleGateway.com or BlueLetterBible.org to find scriptures on that topic and then reword them into prayers from your own heart.

Are you ready to get started?

Let's start with a prayer.

Lord, I thank You for each person who reads this book and lifts up these prayers to You. I pray that You would do a mighty work in their hearts as they spend these next 21 days in prayer with You. Change them from the inside out through Your Word and prayer. Give them a hunger and thirst for You that will continue past the last page of this book. We love You and thank You for this opportunity to come to You with our prayers of gratitude.   Amen.

"Pray without ceasing."
~ I Thessalonians 5:17 (NIV)

"Ask, and it will be given to you; seek, and you will find; knock, and it will be opened to you."
~ Matthew 7:7 (NIV)

"Be anxious for nothing, but in everything by prayer and sup-plication, with thanksgiving, let Your requests be made known to God; and the peace of God, which surpasses all understanding, will guard Your hearts and minds through Christ Jesus."
~ Philippians 4:6-7 (NKJV)

PRAYER OF GRATITUDE #1: GRACE

Lord, today I want to thank You for Your grace. Grace is simply getting something good I do not deserve. So many times I take Your grace for granted; please forgive me. Open my eyes to see Your grace more clearly in my life. Lord, I ask that You take the blinders off of my spiritual eyes so that I can see all of the gifts You have so graciously given me.

It is by Your grace ALONE that I am saved from eternal punishment, and have the promise that I will be with You in heaven for eternity one day. Thank You for rescuing me from my sin and from the clutches of the evil one, Satan. You died for me so that I could have life and life abundantly. Thank You for Your sacrifice.

Thank You for giving me life each new day. When I wake up in the morning, empower me to focus my first thoughts on You. As I lay my head on the pillow at night, remind me of all that You have given me that day. Show me the gifts You have given me and empower me to say a simple, "thank You" back to You.

Thank You for Your amazing grace. Without it, I would be in a hopeless situation. But, because of Your grace, I have so much to be thankful for today and every day.

I love You, Lord. Amen.

"Every good gift and every perfect gift is from above, and comes down from the Father of lights, with whom there is no variation or shadow of turning."
~ James 1:17 (NKJV)

"For by grace you have been saved through faith, and that not of yourselves; it is the gift of God."
~ Ephesians 2:8 (NKJV)

"The thief does not come except to steal, and to kill, and to destroy. I have come that they may have life, and that they may have it more abundantly."
~ John 10:10 (NKJV)

"May grace (God's favor) and peace (which is perfect well-being, all necessary good, all spiritual prosperity, and freedom from fears and agitating passions and moral conflicts) be multiplied to you in [the full, personal, precise, and correct] knowledge of God and of Jesus our Lord."
~ 2 Peter 1:2 (AMPC)

This was an excerpt from the book, 21 Prayers of Gratitude: Overcoming Negativity Through the Power of Prayer and God's Word.

Read all 21 prayers here:

Kindle: http://www.amazon.com/dp/B009KUE87W

Print: http://www.amazon.com/dp/0615917860

GET FREE CHRISTIAN BOOKS

Love getting FREE Christian books online? If so, sign up to be notified of new Christian book promotions and never miss out. Then, grab a cup of coffee and enjoy reading the free Christian books you download.

You will also get our FREE report, "How to Find Free Christian Books Online" that shows you 7 places you can get new books for free!

Sign up here:
www.bodyandsoulpublishing.com/freebooks

Happy reading!

ABOUT SHELLEY HITZ

Shelley Hitz and her husband, CJ, enjoy sharing God's Truth through their speaking engagements and their writing. They enjoy spending time outdoors running, hiking, and exploring God's beautiful creation.

To find out more about Shelley and contact her about speaking at your next event in person or online, go to her website at www.ShelleyHitz.com.

Note from the Author: Reviews are gold to authors! If you have enjoyed this book, would you consider reviewing it on Amazon.com? Thank you!

OTHER BOOKS BY SHELLEY HITZ

Broken Crayons Still Color

A Life of Gratitude

A Life of Faith

Forgiveness Formula

Self-Publishing Books 101

Procrastination to Publication

Calligraphy for Beginners

Brush Strokes Workbook

And many more!

See the entire list here: www.ShelleyHitz.com

OTHER RESOURCES FROM SHELLEY HITZ

For Writing: Shelley is an author coach and has many resources for writers and authors.

Writing Week: a free 7-day writing challenge. Get started here: www.writingweek.com

Free Training: get all her free training for authors here: www.trainingauthors.com/free

For Creativity: Shelley is an artist and teaches online art classes.

Get started with three free classes here: www.yourcreativeadventure.com/free